Ann Herbert Scott

One Good Horse
A COWPUNCHER'S COUNTING BOOK

Pictures by Lynn Sweat

Greenwillow Books, New York

Pencil and transparent oil paints
were used for the full-color art.
The text type is Italia.
Text copyright © 1990 by Ann Herbert Scott
Illustrations copyright © 1990 by Lynn Sweat
from the Publisher, Greenwillow Books, a division of William
Morrow & Company, Inc., 105 Madison Avenue, New York, N.Y. 10016.
Printed in Singapore by Tien Wah Press
First Edition   10 9 8 7 6 5 4 3 2 1

Library of Congress Cataloging-in-Publication Data
Scott, Ann Herbert.
One good horse : a cowpuncher's counting book /
by Ann Herbert Scott ; pictures by Lynn Sweat.
p.   cm.
Summary: While a cowboy and his son check the
cattle, they count the things that they see.
ISBN 0-688-09146-6.   ISBN 0-688-09147-4 (lib. bdg.)
[1. Cowboys—Fiction.   2. Ranch life—Fiction.
3. Counting.]   I. Sweat, Lynn, ill.   II. Title.
PZ7.S4150m 1990   [E]—dc 19   89-1984   CIP
AC

FOR THE MARCHETTI FAMILY OF RATON, NEW MEXICO—
COWPUNCHERS ALL—A. H. S.

FOR MY GRANDSON, CHRISTOPHER—L. S.

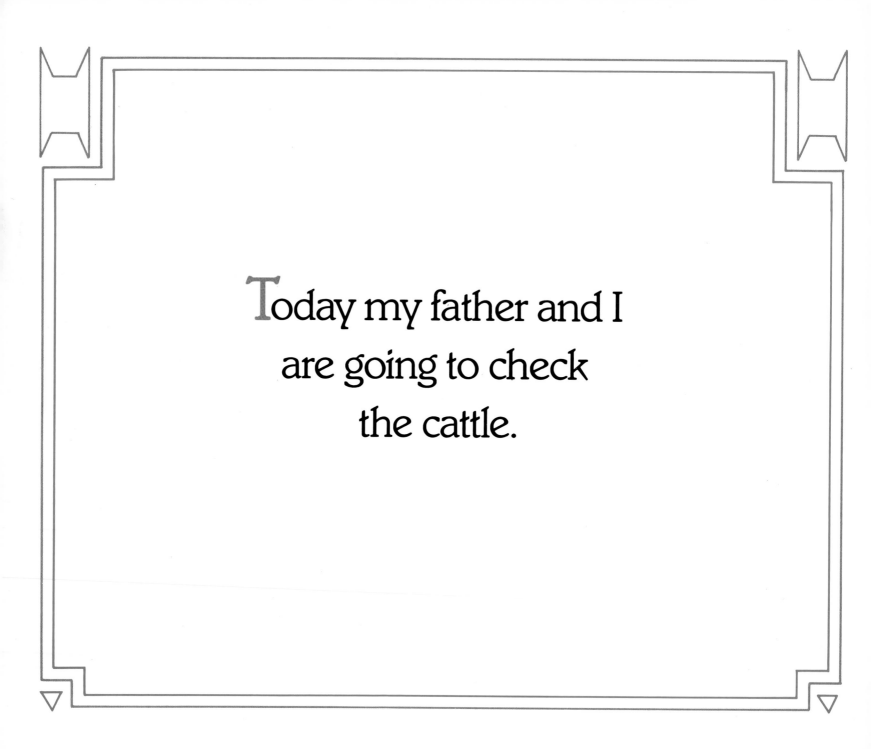

Today my father and I
are going to check
the cattle.

One good horse.

Two buckaroos.

Three cow dogs.

Four old bulls.

Five mother cows.

Six baby calves.

Seven circling

crows.

Eight clumps
of sagebrush.

Nine tall pine trees.

Ten mountain quail.

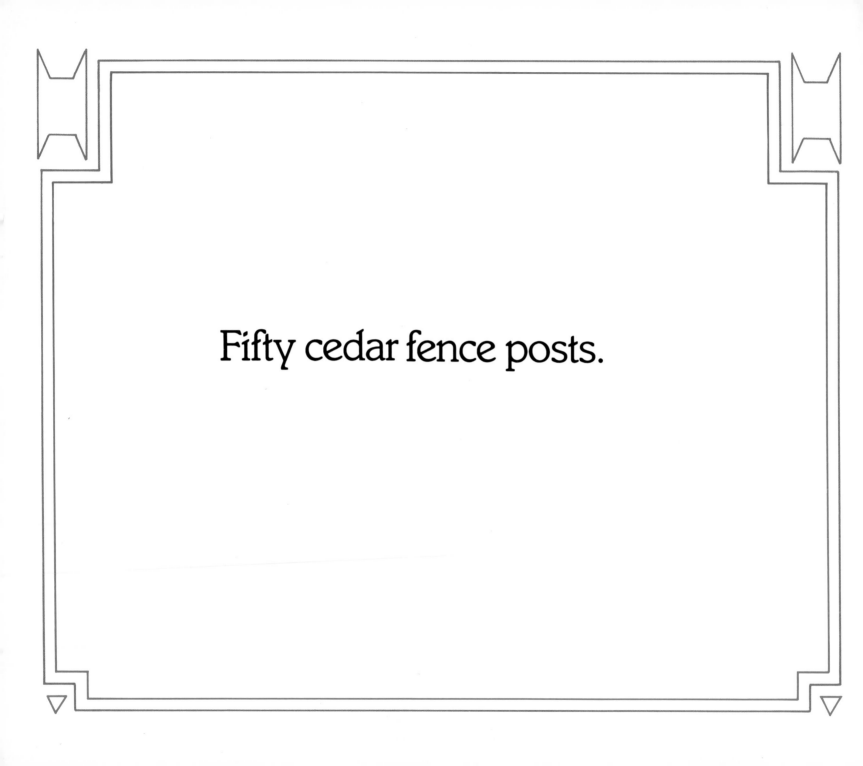

Fifty cedar fence posts.

One hundred head of cattle

grazing in the meadow.